NO MORE SECOND CHANCES

poems to heal your heart

a collection by
CHIARA MASON

Chiara Mason
NO MORE SECOND CHANCES
TSPA The Self Publishing Agency Inc.
Copyright © 2024 by Chiara Mason
First Edition

Softcover ISBN   978-1-7388161-5-6
Hardcover ISBN   978-1-7388161-3-2
eBook ISBN   978-1-7388161-4-9

All rights reserved under International and Pan-American Copyright Conventions. Manufactured in Canada.

No part of this publication may be reproduced, stored in, or introduced into a retrieval system, transmitted in any form or by any means (electronic, mechanical, photocopying, recording, or otherwise), and/or otherwise used in any manner for purposes of training artificial intelligence technologies to generate text, including, without limitation, technologies that are capable of generating works in the same style or genre as this publication, without the prior written permission of the publisher. This book is sold subject to the condition that it shall not, by way of trade or otherwise, be lent, resold, hired out, or otherwise circulated without the publisher's prior written consent in any form of binding, cover, or condition other than that in which it was published.

Book Design | Tracy Hetherington
Chapter Graphic Collages | Tracy Hetherington
Editor | Elise Volkman
Bio Photo | Kayley Bourcier
Publishing Management | TSPA The Self Publishing Agency, Inc.

To those who are hurting —

from a romantic relationship, from a friendship, from family or from your own mental health —

I hope this collection allows you to heal.

Your time of giving out second chances ends now. It's time to choose yourself.

CONTENTS

PLAYLIST   3

LOVESTRUCK   5
the ones I fell for

HEARTBREAK   57
those who left me in pieces

LOVE SCORNED   109
a study in female rage

HEALING   161
stitching myself back together

DEAR READER   213

ACKNOWLEDGEMENTS   215

PLAYLIST

I believe music is simply another form of poetry, so I created a playlist to capture the essence of each feeling explored in this collection. Listen to these songs in advance of reading each section to prepare yourself for the emotions to come, or listen while you read for a multi-sensory experience!

LOVESTRUCK

Enchanted (Taylor's Version) — *Taylor Swift*
this is what falling in love feels like — *JVKE*
Stupid Love — *Dan + Shay*
Burning Desire — *Lana Del Rey*

HEARTBREAK

Death By A Thousand Cuts — *Taylor Swift*
enough for you — *Olivia Rodrigo*
All Too Well (Taylor's Version) — *Taylor Swift*
loml — *Taylor Swift*

LOVE SCORNED

Is It Over Now? (Taylor's Version) — *Taylor Swift*
vampire — *Olivia Rodrigo*
someone like me — *Njomza*
Feather — *Sabrina Carpenter*

HEALING

Now That We Don't Talk (Taylor's Version) — *Taylor Swift*
Radio — *Lana Del Rey*
Flowers — *Miley Cyrus*
just like magic — *Ariana Grande*

LOVESTRUCK

the ones I fell for

I never had the moment of
Love at first sight,
Until I met you.
One look was all it took;
I was captivated.

Your smile, your eyes, your laugh...
They draw me in, until
You are irresistible.
I know exactly what's happening.
I wish I could stop it — but there's no way.
All I can do is sit here and wait
For me to finally finish f a l l i n g
For you.

I spend my afternoons imagining,
Caught up in daydreams
Of what it would be like
For me to be yours.

Sometimes there is an instant connection
That cannot be denied.
Some things are simply too powerful
To be a coincidence.

Persistently, thoughts of you
Invade my mind.
It seems I can't let you go —
Even though you aren't mine at all.
I can't help but wonder,

                        What if?

After my first kiss,
You were the first person I called.
I think deep down I knew:
It should've been you,
But it never got that far with us.

I remember standing next to you
As we watched the show,
Swaying to the music.
Something about the moment stays in my mind...
I should've kissed you then.

The smell of you still lingers:
I close my eyes and
You're right there again,
Next to me.
It's as if no time has passed at all.

You laughed and I saw
All of the stars in the galaxy
Sparkling in your eyes.
In that moment,
I never wanted to let you go.

My heart doesn't belong to me anyway
It's yours

Every time I look at you,
I feel sparks.
When you look back at me,
We're the only ones in the room.

The first time I looked at you,
I was hit by a
tidal wave.

Maybe not the good kind...
Thoughts of you
swim around

                                    in my head:

One minute I'm into you,
The next I think we're better off friends.

I'm sick and tired of listening to my head.
To logic, to sense, to reason.
I'm sick and tired of worrying about
If we'll work, and what others will think —
Because that shouldn't matter.
What should matter are feelings: mine and yours.
I shouldn't be comparing feelings now to past feelings.
I shouldn't be faking love, or denying love,
Or hiding love.
I have to rely on my true, raw feelings —
And I have to believe in love.
Because if I don't have that, I have nothing.
Don't think, *feel*.

I've had my share of heartbreaks,
And now I'm sure with all my heart and soul
That I'm ready for the real thing.

You're all I can think about.
Your eyes are soulful and
Your laugh is music to my ears.
I know this is special:
You listen and you understand.
Somehow, it feels like we've known
Each other forever —
In you, I see my twin flame.

Everything that you are
Is perfect.
You make me feel safe.
You're not like the rest of them —
You broke the cycle.

When I don't want to break down,
I can run to you
Knowing you'll hold me in your arms…
The world will fade away, and
You'll say that everything is okay.

I always used to follow the popular crowd,
Let them take me where they want to go.
I wanted to be someone else, not me,
Until you came into my life.
You showed me who I could be,
If only I would believe.

Isn't that what love is about?
To go, blind, never knowing what to expect?
To make mistakes, for better or worse?
Love is about going for
What makes your heart race.
It's the thrill of going through

                      Something unexpected.

Have you ever been in a crowd of hundreds of people,
Yet never felt more alone?
Have you ever felt your whole life crumbling
Beneath your feet,
And had no idea how to stop it?
Have you ever had a time in your life
When nothing was right,
When everything was wrong?
Have you ever just wanted to forget about everything,
Break down and cry?
I have, and every time my world turns ugly,
I will always turn to you.

If it means we'd get the chance,
I'd put up with it all for you.

Ours was a friendship
Misunderstood by most,
But deep and meaningful for us;
Punctuated by long nights and daily texts,
Yet ripped apart by unrequited love.
Nowadays, when the wee hours meet me again,
I miss those old moments with you.

You saw me in the dress,
And I think you might've lost your breath
For a second —
But maybe I imagined it...
Perhaps in another life,
Something would have happened,
But in this one
Friendship is as far as things will go.

I thought we had more
Maybe I imagined it all

You look the exact same.
If I close my eyes,
I can still hear your laugh in my head,
Like my very own sweet lullaby.

We kissed once and that
Was enough.
I guess it wasn't meant to be.

I wonder if you ever think about me
As the one you lost

With a twelve-year age gap
Most people saw it as wrong —
But we never did.
It never felt wrong for us.

On the heels of my parents' divorce,
I ran away from everything,
Right into your arms —
Slamming the door shut behind me,
So no one else could reach us.

You were magnetic
And I couldn't resist.
I did my best, but
Sometimes

        My body took control,
        My mind faltered,
        Refusing to think of the potential
        Consequences of my actions.

I had to concentrate on my breathing
So it wouldn't stop.
I felt my face flush and
Hoped that no one noticed.

I'm starving for attention
Someone fuel me please

I've tread the lines of morality before
Tip-toeing along, not wanting to lose my balance...
But taking this step would've crossed it,
Too far to be brought back.

For years, I was right on the edge —
But we never got to the point
Of crossing that line.

My desire runs through me,
Takes over me, captivates me.
I'm going crazy with
Hopeless longing...
Without you, I'm nothing.
I would cross oceans for you —
Tell me you'd do the same.

I simply can't stay away;
I can't get you out of my head...
If I could have just one wish
I'd wish that we had never stopped.

I always knew
That we couldn't be anything more
But that didn't discourage me from trying.

I tried to stop myself from

                catapulting over the line,

But I couldn't.

Now I don't know why I did it —
And I'll forever be haunted by the memories.

My heart races when I see you and
Drops into my stomach
Now your fingers brush my leg and
I know I'm in way over my head
Your hand is on my knee and
I edge my arm closer to yours
Your hand finds mine
I can feel you breathing next to me
You pull me closer and
You press your forehead against mine
I don't want you to stop

Tell me about your feelings,
And if you felt as I did —
Tell me why you never acted on it.
    - I know you knew

Why did you lean into our connection
And, the minute I left,
Break it completely?

You'll always be
The one that never was,
The one who slipped away,
The one who never will be.

There are only so many coincidences
Before you're forced to consider
The role of fate:
Perhaps the world has thrown us together
For something bigger than us.

We could have made it
If we had only chosen
To give each other a chance
    – *Missed opportunities*

If they asked me,
"Who was the one who got away?"
I would say it was you —
And I should've tried harder
For what could've been.

Years later,
We both stood on the stage,
Together.
I'm not sure if it was their way
Of trying to pull us back together
After everything that
t o r e us a p a r t.

Over the course of the summer,
We fell madly in love.
In our own little bubble,
Nothing could touch us.

Undeniably we both know
We belong together.
With a year under our belt,
I've never loved you —
Or maybe anyone —
More.
We move into an apartment together;
It's you and me against the world.
We're two years in now and
Sometimes it feels like we will
Last forever.

We would have met at the right time
Our wants would have matched up
I would have been ready
You would have been healed
We could have been happy
And you'd still be here
    – *In another life*

Thoughts swirl around in my head.
I've known the answer all along,
But I don't want to.
Knowing sucks even more than not-knowing does.
Now I see what has always been clear —
I just don't want to admit it to myself.

You are my constant:
It's you.
It's always been you.
I pushed my feelings aside for you before,
And I can't do it again.
I just found you —
I don't want to lose you yet.

HEARTBREAK
those who left me in pieces

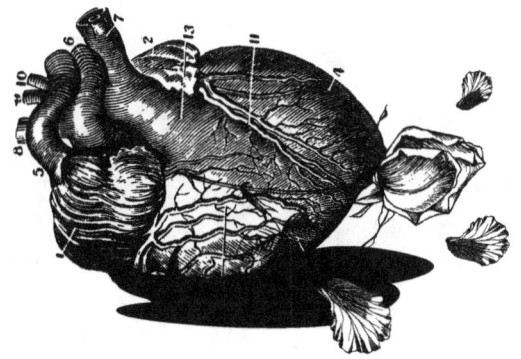

I can never imagine
A life of mine without you —
Even the thought of it
Scares me to death.

No amount of time with you
Will ever be enough

The panic sets in:
Hot tears rise to the surface,
And stream down my face.
I'm not ready to say goodbye.

One moment of potentially losing you
Puts me right back to where I was —
Years ago,
When panic attacks were a regular occurrence,
And I couldn't find my way out.
One moment was all it took and
I'm in that same exact spot again.
It's like nothing has changed at all.

The minute I started to imagine a life
Of mine without you
I knew it was over.

The feeling starts in my chest,

                Then rises to my throat.

Before I know it, I'm hyperventilating.

                I can't get enough air

The world feels on tilt

                I have to sit down before

It all falls apart

                – Panic attack

I have a panic attack in our kitchen,
Telling you I have the overwhelming desire
To leave — not you, but where I am.
Months later, after mulling it over
Again and again in my mind,
I keep circling the same conclusion:
I had to let you go.

If there wasn't such a big age gap,
Maybe it wouldn't matter if I waited…
But I couldn't bear to make you wait years
For something you've always known you wanted…
So we decided to say goodbye.

We were together every moment until I left.
You drove me to the airport;
I cried during the entire flight.
I questioned over and over if it was the right call —
And I couldn't

       find the answer.

I'm screaming
But no one hears me

I'm trying so hard to move on,
But every time I hear from you,
The pain comes rushing back.
I have panic attacks once a month —

                              Collapsing to my floor,
                              Crying my eyes out,
                              Struggling to breathe.

I can't see a way out.

I deeply appreciate your friendship,
But it's still a challenge for me
To figure out how we move forward.

I was away when the crumbling happened
So when the final blow hit,
It hit me like a bus.
Instantly, I knew it was over.
One of you left that day,
And that was when my entire world
As I knew it changed.

Maybe the sick feeling I got in my stomach
Whenever I thought about you was a warning,
Not butterflies.
I guess it was all for the best...
You were destined to break my heart —
I should've known.
I never should've let it get this far.

I still can't tell who was the one
Who let it crumble, me or you.
I'm sure some of it is on me because
I pushed you away —
But a lot of the time, I don't think
We ever should have been friends
In the first place.

Wasn't it silly of me
To think that this time
Would be any different?

I haven't heard from you in months;
Guess our friendship never really mattered much.

After all the things you said,
Did they just mean nothing to you?
I would have done anything for you —
Why did you change your mind?

I'm looking back on all the times we had,
And I still don't understand — what happened to us?
I had always wondered if we would make it,
Now I know we never will.

In the depths of my mind
And deep in my heart,
I think there's a piece of me
Still hoping
You'll come to your senses and
Change your mind.

Everything I've done...
Yet still,
It's not enough.

Six months ago, it was your birthday.
I made such a big deal about it,
Trying to make it special.
A couple months later,
You unexpectedly decided to leave.
Four months later, it's my birthday now —
And you can't even be bothered
To shoot me a text of well wishes.
Guess this is what happens when
Love isn't reciprocated.

It breaks my heart
That you are no longer mine

You showed me the signs,
But I didn't want to see them.
You told me why,
But I didn't want to listen.

What you broke in a moment
I'll spend a lifetime putting back together.
We were never supposed to end up this way —
Now neither of us gets what we want.

Unfortunately our story
Doesn't have a happy ending:
Our love is lost,
But never forgotten.

I throw myself into work as a distraction,
So I don't have to face my own pain.
I try to see someone else,
But I can't do it.
Despite what I try,
I'm still desperately in love with you.

Knowing that you
Don't want to be with me
Really fucking hurts

I can't believe
You didn't even try to fight for me

I care for you so deeply,
But you don't care at all.
So now I have to force myself
To find a way to move on.

There's still songs I can't listen to
Because they remind me of you

I sob in the shower,
Finally letting it out —
It's so damn exhausting
Pretending to be fine.

Sometimes it feels like I'm just empty.

                              There's nothing inside.

You tap on my chest cavity where my heart should be,

                              But it isn't there.

Instead of a heartbeat,

                    the empty space echoes —

                              I'm a hollow shell.

I draw the curtains and
Crawl back into bed,
Refusing to let even the possibility
Of light in.
Today, I don't want to move.
I'll happily be swallowed up
By my melancholy.

I'm going through the motions
Drinking every night to take the edge off
My depression is over me like a haze
And grief clouds my brain

Everything is different
Now that you're gone.
Deep down I know:
I'll never be the same.

I can't do anything else,
So I pour all my grief onto the page
And hope to make it out the other side.

The pain of losing you
Never goes away.
Sometimes it feels like it didn't really happen,
As if it was all a bad dream.

It doesn't matter how much time passes,
I still ache all over.
It doesn't matter where I go,
The loneliness follows me everywhere.
It doesn't matter what I do,
It still feels like it will
Never be enough.

I imagined how things would be different —
But they aren't.
So I have to deal with the now.

It's been nearly a decade since we fell in love,
Over seven years since we ended it,
And three years since you left forever.
Regardless of the amount of time that passes,
The agony will never disappear.

Here I sit,
Trying to figure out how to heal
From this grief that I know will never go away...
Sometimes I wish our story ended differently —
But I'm still grateful we had a story at all.
We were together for only a short time,
Yet I know:
I'll spend the rest of my life missing you.

In another life,
I choose differently
And give us a happy ending
Instead of losing our love.

Sometimes I want to stay
In the sadness.
It reminds me that
You were real,
And what we had was real too.

Five years ago, we celebrated my birthday together —
You decorated our apartment with
Streamers and balloons.

Five years later, I celebrate alone —

Your absence a ●hole in my heart.

Frozen in time
The past still lingers
Like a bad habit
I CAN'T SHAKE.

I still think about it sometimes.
I wish I could go back.
There's so much I would change.

You wanted to leave the door open, but
I decided I had to close it.
I need to find some way to move on...
Now, it's my turn to say goodbye.

Perhaps the only way to know peace
Is to be alone —
But damn, that's lonely.

It's just now occurred to me:
Maybe I don't know what love is
At all

LOVE SCORNED

a study in female rage

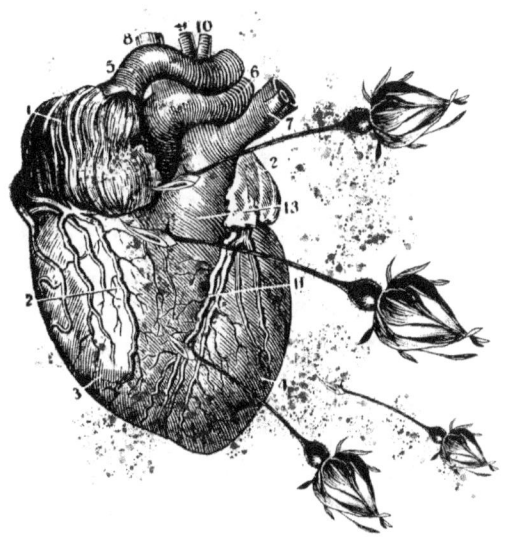

I gave you so many chances
For me to be yours.
I wanted it so badly,
But you could never take the next step.
One day, you'll regret it —
You missed your chance.

I know you felt something, but
You never admitted it.
After I shared my truth,
You went crawling back to her.
You're nothing more than a coward.

All I needed
Was for you to show up —
And you couldn't even do that.

I was madly in love with you,
But you didn't care.
I would have done anything for you,
But it didn't matter.
Eventually I had to choose myself —
The moment I did, you went back to her.
Now you're married,
But it still hurts.

You never reciprocated the love I gave you.
I hate that it took me so long to realize it.

I let my walls down for you.
Don't worry, I won't make
The same mistake again.

You didn't mean any of it.
When are you going to stop playing games?
You confirmed my worst nightmare.
Now, we won't ever happen again.

You screwed me up so much that
I'm now always looking for the worst in people,
Believing that they will leave
Without the slightest bit of proof.

I'm not a toy
For you to play with

You had your chance
You blew it
Now I'm gone
  —*No more second chances*

Don't come running
Back to me
As if nothing's changed —
That's not how this works.

You make me feel hard to love,
And that's not what I deserve.
I deserve someone
Who actually wants to be with me,
And who shows me that
Every damn day.

You don't get to be half in.

I'm not interested in anything half-ass
Or something only convenient for you.
You don't get to decide
When you can show up,
When to walk in and out of my life,
When to be present or ignore me.
I want the commitment and consistency
Of someone who wants to be here,
In the good and the bad.
I'm all in, and I expect
The same from you.
    – All or nothing

I refuse to give you the pleasure of
Me being yours
Unless you have actually committed
To being mine

I'm sick and tired of letting men
Get away with their bullshit.
I'm not going to stick around,
Caring so deeply for you,
When you don't care at all.
This isn't a one-way street —
If you're not going to play your part,
Then I'm out.
   – It takes two, me and you

Being a part of my life
Is a damn privilege
That I'm happy to revoke at any time
If you step out of line.

I will not wait around for you to decide
You should know if you want to be here.

Why are you hovering around,
Buzzing like a bee,
If you don't truly want
A relationship with me?

I've lost people that I thought
I couldn't live without —
So at this point, I'll be just fine
On my own.

I don't need you
I can do myself better anyway
    – *Sex*

I've been saying it all this time.
You would have known,
If you'd been paying attention.

If you continue to cross my boundaries,
I will cut you off.
Don't act so surprised when it happens —
You handed me the damn scissors.

I refuse to apologize for cutting you off.
I give a lot of chances —
If we're at this point, you took it too far.
It's true what they say:
Karma is a real bitch.

Losing me
Is your punishment

I don't know what delusional world
You live in.

                    I see right through your lies.

You're full of shit.
I'm putting my foot down, finally —
I don't deserve this.

Take responsibility
For your fucking actions.
You aren't absolved of all guilt.

Your blatant lies and denial,
Twisting of the truth,
Manipulation and confusion —
It all ends now.
  – *Stop the gaslighting*

You can't fool me
With your bag of tricks.
We've been down this road before —
I know exactly how this ends.

Don't project your shit on me,
And try to make it my fault —
I am not responsible for your
Emotions, aggressiveness, or lack of boundaries.
Check yourself and
GO TO FUCKING THERAPY.

Stop catering to the men in your life
Let them cater to you for once
You deserve respect
At bare minimum
 – *To all women*

Expecting women to give you something
In return for being a "nice" guy
Is bullshit.
Drop your fucking expectations.
We can make our own decisions and
We're allowed to change our minds,
Whenever we choose.

If I don't hear from you
In over a month,
We're not friends.
I'm moving on.

If you don't have the ability
To take 2 seconds and text me back
Then you aren't "too busy" —
You just don't want to.
    – *Say it like it is*

Friends don't date other friends' exes
You should've known better —
Or maybe I should've,
For trusting you at all.

I know how to bury the hatchet,
But I can sure as hell
DIG ONE UP
When I need to.

Don't tell me you care
When you're putting in zero effort
To prove it.
Words mean nothing
Until your actions back them up.

When it all goes up in flames,
Just remember:
You had the match

                          and chose to light it.

This one's on you.

I didn't have to do a single thing —
All I did was step back and watch.
You destroyed it all yourself.

Don't manipulate and abuse me,
Then try to tell me you love me —
Your actions show that you don't.
Good people do not
Emotionally abuse
The people they supposedly "love."

What will be enough for you?
Getting on my knees to beg?
Agreeing with everything you say?
Hailing you as the almighty?
Absolving you of everything you've done?
I don't fucking think so.
  – *Taking my worth back*

You can't distract me by
Hurling your insults.
I know what's true and what isn't,
And I choose to stand in my truth.

I'll keep my dignity
While yours falls down
And we get to see the real you
   – *Coward*

I've finally decided
You're not worthy.
I'm not yours anymore.
I deserve a hell of a lot better
Than you.

I'll stand up for myself,
Even when it hurts to stand my ground —
I won't back down.
You're not allowed to walk all over me anymore.

I am so angry and disappointed
In myself
For choosing to accept so little.

I'm taking back what's mine
It belongs to me
You will not be the thief
Of my joy anymore
   – *Screw you, depression*

You will not get the luxury
Of watching me evolve
Into the next stage of life

This is the last time
I accept what I don't deserve

I can choose the ending,
Because I am the creator
Of my own damn life.

It's time
To save myself

HEALING

stitching myself back together

I've been waiting my whole life
For someone to choose me.
Over and over and over,
They never do.
I'm done waiting:
I'm choosing my damn self.

I've given so much of myself away:
My love, energy, resources, time,
All to people and things —
But none to myself.
So I'm changing the course,
And re-investing it all back into me.
Because who's a better investment
Than myself?
I know I can bet on her.

I'm so sick and tired
Of giving everything I have to people
And getting nothing in return.
It's exhausting,
So I'm not doing it anymore.

I'm not living to please anyone
But myself.
The people-pleaser in me
Is done.

Everyone thinks I chose this —
But the truth is, you left me no choice.
After the manipulation and abuse,
If I wanted to survive,
My only choice was leaving.

Love shouldn't dim your light
It should make it shine brighter
   – *Choose the light*

I lost a whole lot of people
When I chose to stand up for myself

I'll never be enough for you —
But as long as I'm enough for me,
That's all that matters.

The vulnerability leaves me exposed
But I choose not to shy away —
My emotional and deep connection
Is what makes me unique.
I will not apologize for it,
Just because you can't feel at all.

I'm standing up for myself,
Believing in what I have to offer,
And creating the life I deserve.

Clear and consistent communication,
Mutual effort,
Strong boundaries —

        That's my love language.

You are worthy of effort
You deserve to be desired
You have a right to a love that doesn't leave you
Confused or hurt
   – A message to my past self

I'm not giving out second chances.
I'm no longer forcing myself to do things
I don't actually like.
I'm not settling for the bare minimum,
Or sacrificing parts of myself
To get nothing in return.

I will choose myself,
Over and over and over —
Until it's no longer a choice,
It's simply a habit.

The most terrifying thought is
Believing I've already wasted
My potential

The only person I'm up against
Is myself.

Even when I'm struggling,
I am still worthy

I don't need to do it all,
I just need to live and survive —
And I can choose what that looks like.

Investing in what makes me happy
Is never a waste of my time.
Even if it seems strange to others,
I am the one responsible for my happiness —
And I will do whatever it takes
To create that happiness.

There's so many who don't make it this far.
I owe it to all of them
To keep going,
And live the most fulfilling life possible.
Time is too precious
To let it pass me by.

The world seemed to continue,
Even though I was irrevocably changed.
Since everything inside of me had changed,
I felt everything on the outside must too.
Time suddenly felt priceless,
And I didn't want to waste
A damn second.

I will make as many mistakes as I can,
Taste different things,
See new sites that fill me with wonder,
Change directions a million times,
Let myself fall in love and get heartbroken —
Truly feel and experience it all.
I want this life to be as full as possible,
Because it's mine.
  – *We only get one life*

If I can't find what I'm looking for,
Then maybe I need to create it
For myself.

Does it make me
                    selfish
To pursue a path entirely my own?

An uncertain — but I believe fulfilling — route?

Or does it make me
                    brave
To give everything up in the belief of something

Truly right for me?

I don't know if I'm ready,
But sometimes we don't know
Until we try.

The only thing I can do to process
Everything scattered around in my brain
Is to write and create.
It's the only way for me to
Make sense of the world.
I can't find a way forward without it —
So I'm no longer forcing myself to try.

I'm tuning in to my creative energy,
And tuning out the self-doubt.
Believing in what I'm doing now,
Rather than worrying about the future.
I'll keep going, despite all odds.
I believe life can be extraordinary,
If we choose to make it that way.

No one else can make me happy,
So I have to do it for myself.
Nothing will fill that void inside —
Only self-love.

I will hold onto the belief
That I can create a life I love —
I just need the courage to
Go after it.

Piece by piece,
I'll solve the puzzle
And make myself whole.

I hope you're watching
Looking down on me
And really fucking proud
    – I hope heaven is wonderful to you

I am getting back to
My joy.
I wish it had never left in the first place —
Though perhaps I needed this push
To get my joy back.

Sometimes I just need the little things:
The sun on my face,
The waves crashing on the shore,
Being surrounded by green space.
Bit by bit,
They stitch me back together.

I will not
Wait to live my own life
Because someone hasn't joined me.
I will go on my own adventures,
Because my own company is valuable.

We only have a limited time together:
I'm not going to waste it
By trying to run away,
When instead I could be here,
With all of you —
Enjoying the time we have left.
In moments like these,
I know I made the right decision.
I will never regret
Being here and enjoying
The time we have together.
   - Family is precious

I hope you find ways
To enjoy the things you used to,
Before they told you to give it up.
  – *Healing your inner child*

Turns out, I just needed to believe in myself —
All along, that was the key
To opening the next door
And stepping into the light.

How I'm healing:

- Dancing around the house
- Singing at the top of my lungs
- Exploring new places
- Getting out in nature
- Going to therapy
- Creating and expressing myself
- Setting strong boundaries
- Prioritizing myself
- Doing what makes me happy

The only thing I care about
Is making my younger self proud.
She deserves this.

I've come to realize that
Having a community and safe space
Is more important than anything.
Now I'm determined to make mine.

I was addicted to escaping
For a long time.
It was fun…
Until it wasn't anymore.
Somewhere along the way,
I realized I needed to stop running
If I ever wanted to be at peace.

I always wish that they would stay
But I'm not much better myself:
I've never been in one spot long enough
To fully plant roots —
So maybe, I'm the one to blame.

The losses are always lessons
And more often than not, they're blessings:
Showing you exactly what you don't want,
And leading you closer to what you truly desire.
   – *Learn the lessons and move forward*

I don't know where I got the idea
That it was weak to do things with others.
I thought it made me so special,
That I could do everything on my own.
But that simply isn't true —
We don't make it on our own.
Our lives are built by those we're intertwined with.
I never would've gotten here by myself;
A whole damn village helped me find the way.

I'm kicking myself for wasting this time
When all along,
I could have been the one shining
   – I'm the entire universe

My life hasn't turned out
Exactly the way I imagined —
But maybe that's the beauty of it.

I can't quite see what the future holds,
But all I know for sure is
Living a creative life
Makes all the difference.

Sometimes I get glimmers of an old life —
Or perhaps it's one yet to come.

DEAR READER

It has been quite the journey to get here. After releasing my first book in 2023, I had a moment of panic: what if I couldn't write anymore, and I'd used up all my creative energy? I forced myself to sit down and try to write, to see what would happen. Turns out, the minute I put pen to paper, the words kept on coming.

Most of the poems in this collection were written during that time, from mid-2023 to mid-2024. It was a time of big changes and big reflections. I looked back at many of my past relationships and life experiences — romantic relationships, platonic relationships, my relationship with myself — trying to make sense of it all. I also looked towards the future and imagined what it might look like. It felt as if it was changing rapidly right before my eyes.

I still don't quite know what the future holds for me, though every now and then I catch a glimpse of what it could be. What I do know for sure is that writing will always play a role as I move forwards. Writing this collection helped me heal — an effect that writing always seems to have on me. It is for this reason that I will continue to write as life brings new experiences my way.

My hope for you, dear reader, is that reading this collection helps you heal just as much as writing it helped me. These words came at a time when I needed them most, allowing me to take back my worth and to heal my own heart. I hope it does the same for you. My wish is that you recognize your own worth, stop giving out those second chances, and finally find the space to heal. I'm right there with you.

All my love,
Chiara

ACKNOWLEDGEMENTS

I'm lovestruck to have the support of so many wonderful people who brought *No More Second Chances* to life. Many thank-yous ahead!

I must begin with the wonderful team at TSPA — it has been a privilege to work with you again in bringing my second book to life. Two books in and it keeps getting better! You're the only team I'll give many chances to 😊

To Elise, my deeply caring editor — I truly cannot imagine trusting anyone else with editing my words. I endlessly appreciate your care for my work and your approach to editing. Thank you for another successful run together; I'm hoping for more to come!

To Tracy, my inspired designer — I am so grateful to work collaboratively on the visual components of my book together. Your combination of listening to my ideas and suggesting your own to create an incredible end result is truly inspiring. I am very blessed to work with you, and I hope to work together again!

To Ira and Megan, the wheels who keep TSPA turning — thank you for allowing me to take my own approach with book two. I appreciate your trust as I find my way forward creatively. I couldn't reach the finish line without your support!

I don't think I can ever fully express the extent of my gratitude for finding and working with the TSPA team. Thank you, always.

In my personal life, I am lucky to have the support of many. One specific person I want to thank, who played a role in this particular book, is my mom. Mom, you provided me with a safe space to write and edit the bulk of this collection in early 2024. The appreciation I have for being able to do so within your home cannot be overstated. *No More Second Chances* wouldn't have come into being without that safe space to land, and without your support for me to explore my creativity. Thank you, from the bottom of this pieced-back-together heart.

Thank-yous also go to the many local businesses and bookstores who have supported my work. A special thank-you to the team at Indigo Kelowna, who have been incredibly supportive through multiple book signing events. I first had the idea of the concept for *No More Second Chances* at a signing there in February 2024, and a year later, I'm ecstatic that it has come to fruition. Thank you for supporting local authors; it means the world!

Last but not least, to you, dear reader. It would not have been possible for me to launch a second book without your support of my first, *Blooming: Poetry for Seasons of Change*. Thank you for supporting my creative work and allowing me to embrace the dream of being an author! My biggest hope with *No More Second Chances* is that these poems help heal your heart, as they did mine. Thank you for continuing to join me on the journey, and allowing me to become a part of yours.

XO,

Chiara

AUTHOR BIO

Chiara Mason is an award-winning Canadian indie author, multi-passionate creative, and mental-health advocate. You'll often find her jet-setting to explore a new place or practicing the art of wine drinking. She is local to the Okanagan region of BC, Canada.

Her debut book, *Blooming: Poetry for Seasons of Change*, was released in 2023. It was named the 2023 Poetry Winner of The Canadian Book Club Awards and was a 2024 Poetry Finalist in the Next Generation Indie Book Awards. *No More Second Chances* is her second book.

Find more of her work at **chiaragoesglobal.com**.

www.ingramcontent.com/pod-product-compliance
Lightning Source LLC
Chambersburg PA
CBHW071237070526
44583CB00017B/2223